NATIONAL
GEOGRAPHIC

CIVILIZATIONS PAST TO PRESENT

MALI

KEVIN SUPPLES

PICTURE CREDITS
Cover Sandro Vannini/Corbis; page 3 (top) D. Poole/Robert Harding World Imagery; page 3 (bottom) Charles and Josette Lenars/Corbis; pages 4–5, 7 (bottom), 8, 9 (right), 15, 20 (left), 23 Nik Wheeler, Corbis; page 7 (top) Topaloff Boyan/Corbis Sygma; page 9 (left) Eric and David Hosking/Corbis; page 10 Esha Chiocchio; page 11 J. Pate/Robert Harding World Imagery; page 12 Daniel Lainé/Corbis; page 13 (left) Wolfgang Kaehler/Corbis; page 13 (right) Abbas/Magnum; page 14 Georg Gerster/National Geographic Image Collection; page 16 Frances Linzee Gordon/Lonely Planet Images; page 17 (inset) Burt Silverman/National Geographic Image Collection; page 17 (main) Patrick Ben Luke Syder/Lonely Planet Images; page 18 Benito/Corbis Sygma; page 19 (top) Bibliotheque Nationale, Paris, France/Bridgeman Art Library, UK; page 19 (bottom) Chris Rainier/Corbis; page 20 (right) Penny Tweedie/Corbis; page 21 Jason Lauré; page 22 (left) Neal Preston/Corbis; page 22 (right) Royal Pavilion, Libraries and Museums, Brighton; page 24 North Carolina Museum of Art/Corbis.

Produced through the worldwide resources of the National Geographic Society, John M. Fahey, Jr., President and Chief Executive Officer; Gilbert M. Grosvenor, Chairman of the Board; Nina D. Hoffman, Executive Vice President and President, Books and Education Publishing Group.

PREPARED BY NATIONAL GEOGRAPHIC SCHOOL PUBLISHING
Ericka Markman, Senior Vice President and President, Children's Books and Education Publishing Group; Steve Mico, Vice President, Editorial Director; Marianne Hiland, Executive Editor; Anita Schwartz, Project Editor; Jim Hiscott, Design Manager; Kristin Hanneman, Illustrations Manager; Diana Bourdrez, Picture Editor; Matt Wascavage, Manager of Publishing Services; Sean Philpotts, Production Manager.

MANUFACTURING AND QUALITY MANAGEMENT
Christopher A. Liedel, Chief Financial Officer; Phillip L. Schlosser, Director; Clifton M. Brown III, Manager.

PROGRAM DEVELOPMENT
Gare Thompson Associates, Inc.

ART DIRECTION
Dan Banks, Project Design Company

CONSULTANTS/REVIEWERS
Dr. Margit E. McGuire, School of Education, Seattle University, Seattle, Washington

BOOK DEVELOPMENT
Nieman Inc.

BOOK DESIGN
Three Communication Design, LLC

PICTURE EDITING AND MANAGEMENT
Corrine L. Brock

MAP DEVELOPMENT AND PRODUCTION
Bruce Burdick

Published by the National Geographic Society
1145 17th Street, N.W.
Washington, D.C. 20036-4688

ISBN: 0-7922-4539-3

Fourth Printing September 2011
Printed in Canada

Cover: Women walking outside the Great Mosque in Djenné

page 3 (top): Malic children

page 3 (bottom): A headdress shaped like an antelope

CONTENTS

INTRODUCTION

Imagine riding a camel across a desert in Africa. You lead a long line of camels. The camels traveling behind you carry gold. You find your way by studying the sun, the stars, and the wind patterns in the sand.

Or imagine that you copy important books by hand. Month after month, you put Arabic words onto paper with pen and ink. When you are finished, you have made another copy of the book. These are just two of the things that you might have done if you had lived in Mali **long ago**.

The **empire** of Mali was a large, powerful kingdom in West Africa hundreds of years ago. It ruled over much of West Africa. The people of Mali traded gold and other important goods.

Today, Mali is one of many countries in West Africa. It is ruled by a president instead of a king. Some people live much the same way people did in the past. Other people live in large modern cities.

Let's explore the Mali of long ago and the Mali of today. There is much to learn about both of them.

A Mali worker gathers water near onion fields.

MALI: THEN AND NOW

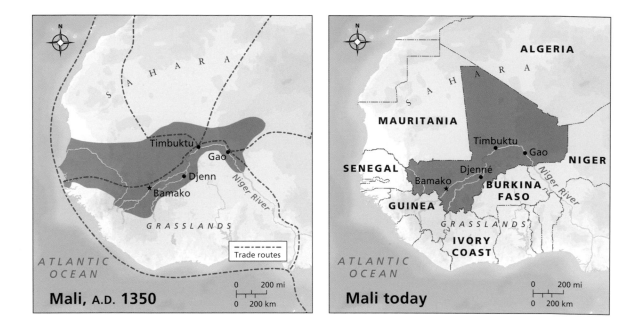

Mali, A.D. 1350

Mali today

Mali is a land of big differences. There are burning hot deserts. There are shady forests. There are cities with buildings of glass and steel. And there are villages with old mud buildings. Giraffes, elephants, and lions roam the grasslands.

Long ago, Mali stretched from the Atlantic Ocean in the west to present-day Niger in the east.

Mali included parts of the Sahara, a desert in the north, and grasslands in the south. Important trade routes crossed through Mali.

Cities in Mali **today** look much like many cities around the world. Families have television sets, electric power, and cars. But in the villages, many people don't have even paved roads. Their villages are like those of **long ago**.

Old buildings in Mali

Modern building on the Niger River in Bamako

Look at the two maps on page 6. Find the Sahara. It is a huge desert that stretches across Africa. Rain doesn't fall very often there. Temperatures can reach 110 degrees Fahrenheit (43 degrees Celsius). Notice that Mali's major cities are on or near the Niger River.

What modern-day cities were also part of the Mali empire? Which city was the capital **long ago** and **today**?

COMMUNITY LIFE

HOUSES

In Mali **long ago**, some people lived in square houses with wooden or reed roofs. Others lived in round houses with cone-shaped roofs made of straw. People sometimes made a roof from the trunk and leaves of palm trees that grew nearby.

Most houses were made from mud bricks. The people mixed clay with water from a nearby river or lake. They made bricks from this mixture. Then they built walls and covered them with a smooth layer of mud.

The houses had one or two stories. They had few windows, and the floors were hard ground. There were no chairs or beds. Families slept on mats. They cooked outside in a small courtyard.

Today, some people in Mali live in houses made from mud bricks. Many people live in houses built of cinder blocks and other modern materials. In cities, people live in tall buildings.

In this small village, some houses have cone-shaped roofs made of straw.

Monkey bread is fruit from the baobab tree.

Women pound grain to make flour.

FARMING AND FOOD

Do you know what monkey bread is? It's the fruit of the baobab tree. Fruits were some of the main foods for most people in Mali **long ago**.

Most people worked as farmers. Men and boys planted the crops. Women and girls weeded and tended the growing plants. Everyone worked together at harvest time. Grains—such as rice, wheat, and **sorghum**—were major foods. Many farmers raised sheep and goats, both for milk and meat. People fished and hunted. They traded extra food for things they needed.

Today, many people in Mali are farmers. Like farmers **long ago**, they grow many kinds of plants. Cotton is an important crop in Mali **today**. **Cassava** is a root that is common food in Mali. It must be cooked enough before you eat it. Otherwise, it can poison you!

Modern farmers raise chickens for both meat and eggs. People often raise cattle, sheep, and goats. They also catch fish. Farmers in Mali grow fruits and peanuts too. Many farmers in Mali don't have modern farm machines. They use hand tools like those from a long time ago. This makes farming hard work.

When the people of Mali began trading **long ago** with people to the north, they learned of the religion of **Islam.** Most people in Mali became **Muslims.** Muslims are people who practice the Islamic religion. Islam is based on the teaching of an Arab **prophet** named Muhammad.

By around the year 1000, many West African rulers, traders, and other people had become Muslims. Many different groups of people lived in the kingdom of Mali. A shared religion and language, Arabic, helped these different groups feel like they were one people.

Muslims worship in buildings called **mosques.** In Mali, people built mosques from the same material used for houses—mud bricks. The people of a town worked together to build and repair a mosque. Some of Mali's mosques are hundreds of years old.

Today, 90 percent of the citizens of Mali are Muslims. About 1 percent are Christians. Many other people, especially those in distant villages, still practice ancient African religions. These religions have forms of worship that developed over hundreds of years.

LOOKING BACK

The people of the city of Djenné (jen-AY) have always repaired their beautiful mosque every year after the rainy season. People work together to spread fresh mud on the walls with their bare hands. The work is done in a single day.

Palm-wood sticks provide an easy way to climb the walls and repair the Great Mosque in Djenné.

Children learn at a school in Mali.

SCHOOL

In Mali **long ago,** big cities had libraries. They also had colleges. Only the sons of the most important people went to these schools. Their teachers were Muslims. The main subjects were religion and the Arabic language.

Most people learned what they needed to know at home. Sometimes, wealthy families sent their sons to one of Mali's cities to learn a trade or craft. They learned from a master craftsperson. Weaving and iron-making were two important and popular jobs. Girls weren't allowed to leave home to study or learn a job.

Several women and children get water at a well in Sangha, Mali.

LOOKING BACK

Before the printing press was invented, all books had to be copied by hand. Books were important in the ancient city of Timbuktu. Some people owned hundreds of books. Most of them were written in Arabic. Many of these books still exist.

In Mali **today,** many children don't go to school. Many people never learn to read or write. Children help take care of the family animals. Most girls learn to cook and weave. They also get water, help with shopping, and take care of younger children in the family. Children who go to school study geography, reading, writing, mathematics, and foreign languages.

TRADE AND TRANSPORTATION

SALT AND GOLD

If you had gone to a market in Mali **long ago,** you might have used chunks of salt as money. Salt was an important Mali trade good. People used it to flavor and preserve food. **Long ago,** salt was costly because it was hard to find.

When seawater **evaporates,** or dries up, it leaves salt behind. The salt forms in hard layers, often underground. Men cut blocks of salt from these layers. Each block weighed about 50 pounds (nearly 23 kilograms). Workers put these blocks on their heads and carried them over land. Then they loaded the blocks onto boats and floated the salt to markets.

Workers unload salt slabs.

LOOKING BACK

People who traded with Mali shared stories about gold. One story told that the people of Mali were so rich that they wore clothes spun from gold! Do you think this was true?

Gold was another important trade good. Miners dug the gold from deep underground. Local traders sold the gold to North Africans, who sold it to people in Europe.

Today in Mali, people transport blocks of salt the same way they did in the past. Gold is mined and sold to other countries. Mali also **exports,** or sells outside its borders, cotton, fish, peanuts, and meat. Food, machinery, and cloth are some of Mali's major **imports,** or goods bought from other countries.

TRADING CENTERS

Guess how people got the news in Mali **long ago**. Traders told them about things in the outside world.

Traders traveled long distances to buy and sell goods. Many trade routes passed through Mali. Small towns along the routes grew into larger trading centers. People came to hear the latest information and buy the newest goods.

Timbuktu was Mali's most famous trading center. It was a busy city of more than 100,000 people. It was called the "Pearl of the Desert."

Today, Timbuktu is a much smaller city. Newer ones, like Bamako, are more important, but tourists go to Timbuktu to walk the narrow streets and see the old buildings. They like to imagine they can still hear the traders telling all the latest news.

A woman sells bread made in a clay oven in Timbuktu.

WORD POWER

Stories tell that a woman called Buctoo guarded the small settlement that became Timbuktu. So, the city was named by combining the woman's name with *tim*, which means "that belongs to."

15

Imagine crossing the shifting sands of the huge Sahara. How will you find your way? There are no roads or highways. The days are brutally hot. Nights are freezing cold. Sometimes, blowing sand makes it impossible to see. You can find water only at a resting place called an **oasis**.

You need a special kind of transportation in the desert. In Mali **long ago**, one animal helped to make transportation possible. It was the camel!

Camels can carry heavy loads over long distances. They can walk 20 to 25 miles (32 to 40 kilometers) each day without stopping for food or water. They can go without water for about a week. Camels can also cross sandy and rocky land easily because their feet are padded.

Mali's traders traveled in large groups called **caravans**. One caravan might have as many as a thousand camels! Camels carried goods, traders, food, and tents.

In Mali **today**, camels and caravans often carry loads. Ships, trucks, trains, and planes carry people and goods also.

LOOKING BACK

At age 10, boys began to care for their family's camels. They had to learn to recognize the brand, or mark, an owner burned into his camels' hides. Boys also learned to identify each camel's tracks in the sand. They learned to pick out their own camels from thousands of others.

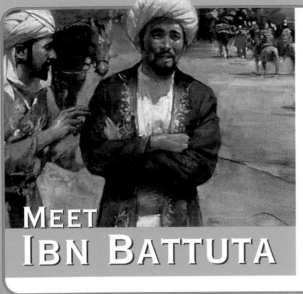

Meet
Ibn Battuta

Much of what we know about early Mali is from the writings of Ibn Battuta (IHB-uhn bah-TOO-tuh). Ibn Battuta was a Muslim from the North African country of Morocco. He traveled for almost 30 years across parts of Africa, Europe, and Asia. In the 1350s, he joined a caravan traveling to Mali. At the end of his life, Ibn Battuta wrote about the places he had seen and the people he had met. He is remembered as one of the world's greatest travelers.

Boats docked on the Niger River

GOVERNMENT

Long ago, a famous king named Sundiata (sun-di-OT-uh) was Mali's first ruler. His name means "hungering lion." Until Sundiata was seven, he could not walk and seldom spoke. As Sundiata grew, he became strong. He learned to hunt, ride, and lead an army.

Sundiata won an important battle in about 1235. A story tells about Sundiata's great victory. It tells how Sundiata killed his enemy with an arrow tipped with the poisoned claw of a rooster. Sundiata conquered various groups of people and brought peace to the area. This was how the kingdom of Mali grew. Sundiata became known as the Lion King.

Other great kings ruled Mali over the next 300 years. In time, however, the kingdom grew weak. Wars were the main cause. Also, most traders no longer went to Mali. It was no longer important in the world. Other nations took control of the country.

France ruled Mali from 1895 until 1958. Then in 1960, the Republic of Mali was formed. **Today,** Mali is an independent country with more than 12 million people. A president, a prime minister, and a national assembly rule Mali. The official language of Mali is French, but other languages are spoken too.

A man votes in 1992. This was the first election for a president in Mali.

MANSA MUSA

ansa Musa led one of the most famous camel caravans ever formed. He was a king who lived in Mali in the 1300s. He was also a Muslim. In 1324, he decided to make a **pilgrimage,** or religious journey, to Mecca. Mecca is a city in Saudi Arabia. The prophet Muhammad was born in Mecca. So, all Muslims are supposed to make a pilgrimage to that city at least once if they can.

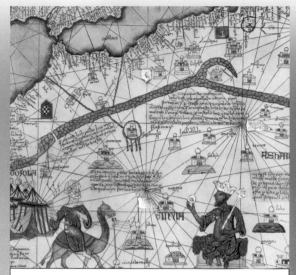

On this old map, Mansa Musa is shown holding a lump of gold.

Mansa Musa's journey lasted a year. Some say that thousands of servants and soldiers traveled with his caravan. Mansa Musa traveled to Egypt. The caravan camped along the Nile River near Cairo (KI-roh), Egypt's capital. At that time, Cairo was one of the world's richest cities.

When Mansa Musa returned to Mali in 1325, he brought new ideas with him. He wanted his people to understand the value of learning. He built colleges for studying religion and law. Soon Mali became a center of learning.

THE ARTS

CRAFTS

Long ago, the people of West Africa made many works of art. They did paintings that told stories. They made fine masks for ceremonies. Sculptors used clay, wood, or metal to make figures of animals and people.

Weaving was an important craft. An old story told how a spider had taught people the magic art of weaving. Many tales and legends tell of spiders in West Africa.

A woodworker carves a spider on a stamp.

The frame for weaving was important. It is called a **loom**. Each part of the loom had meaning. Before starting work, some weavers said a prayer over the loom. People believed that the loom then sang a song that only the weaver could hear.

West Africans gave special honor to blacksmiths. Their craft was thought to be magic because they worked with metal and fire.

Today, tourists buy crafts from Mali. Craftspeople still tell stories through their art.

Two women weave at a large loom.

STORYTELLERS

If you couldn't read or write, how would you remember the history of your country? How would you pass on the traditions of your family? In Mali **long ago**, storytellers known as **griots** (gree-OHS) did this special job.

Griots learned long accounts of important events in the history of Mali. Then they passed these tales on to others. Sometimes, they used music, poetry, drama, and dance to make their stories more lively. They told about heroes and great deeds from Mali's past.

Arab traders first wrote down some of these stories in the 1600s. Modern people know a lot about early Mali from these stories.

Today, griots still tell past events in ancient songs and stories. They often play music or drum as they recite. Their tales remind us of the powerful empire of Mali and the people who made it great. You may have read one of the griot's stories. Many children's books today tell stories from West Africa.

A griot studies fox tracks left in a pattern drawn in the sand.

CONTRIBUTIONS

People around the world enjoy the music of Salif Keita, a pop star from Mali.

Many people around the world have enjoyed the spider tales and music kept alive by griots.

Mali's builders, artists, and sculptors left behind wonderful works of art. Some of it is in museums today. This art inspires modern artists in western Africa and elsewhere. Mali's famous places, especially Timbuktu, continue to thrill explorers, scholars, and travelers from around the world.

The leaders and citizens of Mali made lasting contributions to world culture. Their trade routes across the Sahara connected people from Africa, Asia, and Europe.

For hundreds of years, the countries of Europe got much of their gold from Mali. This continued to be important until the 1500s. At that time, Europeans reached the Americas and found new sources of this precious metal.

LOOKING BACK

In early Mali, musicians played drums, a two-stringed guitar, and a harp-like instrument. Everyone enjoyed singing and dancing.

GLOSSARY

caravan a single line of animals, such as camels, used to move goods and people

cassava a tropical plant with starchy roots. It is good to eat.

empire a group of countries, lands, or peoples under one government or ruler

evaporate to change from a liquid to a vapor, such as mist or smoke

export to send goods for sale out of a country

griot a storyteller in western Africa

imports goods brought in from a foreign country for use or sale

Islam the religion based on the teachings of Muhammad

loom a frame for weaving cloth

mosque a Muslim place of worship

Muslim a person who follows the religion of Islam

oasis a place in a desert where there is water

pilgrimage a journey to some sacred, or holy, place

prophet a religious leader who speaks as the voice of God

sorghum any of a group of tall grass plants. One kind has a sweet juice used for making molasses.

These rock paintings are in a region of cliffs northeast of Djenné.

INDEX

An antelope headpiece